MW00978311

Animals in the Garden

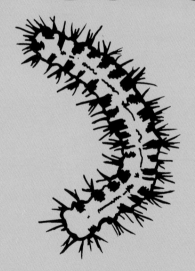

Élisabeth de Lambilly

GARETH**STEVENS**
GS
P U B L I S H I N G
A Member of the WRC Media Family of Companies

The Ant

I am an ant.
I live underground
with thousands of other ants.
I work hard in your garden,
looking for tasty treats
to bring home to share.

The Redbreast

I am a little redbreast.
Have you heard
my cheerful songs?
If you stand very still,
I will hop around your feet,
looking for something
to fill my round tummy.

The Grasshopper

I am a grasshopper.
I make sounds like
tiny bells with my legs.
I am green all over,
like the grass I hide in.
If you try to catch me,
I will disappear
with one flying leap.

The Blackbird

I am a blackbird.
I make my nest in the woods.
When I fly into your garden,
you will see my yellow beak
and my dark feathers.
I am one bird that sings
before the Sun comes up.

The Beetle

I am a beetle.
I wear a black shell.
You might run away
when I crawl by
because I look a little scary.
But I will not hurt you at all.

The Vole

I am a vole.
I look like a little mouse.
I make my nest underground
and sleep there all day.
I love to eat dandelions
in your garden.
I eat all night long.

The Caterpillar

I am a caterpillar.
I move very, very slowly.
Because I have so many feet,
I have to watch
each step I take!
Soon, in my cocoon,
I will become
a beautiful butterfly.

Please visit our Web site at: www.garethstevens.com
For a free color catalog describing Gareth Stevens Publishing's
list of high-quality books and multimedia programs, call
1-800-542-2595 (USA) or 1-800-387-3178 (Canada).
Gareth Stevens Publishing's fax: (414) 332-3567.

Library of Congress Cataloging-in-Publication Data available upon request from publisher.
Fax (414) 336-0157 for the attention of the Publishing Records Department.

ISBN-13: 978-0-8368-7832-5

This edition first published in 2007 by
Gareth Stevens Publishing
A Member of the WRC Media Family of Companies
330 West Olive Street, Suite 100
Milwaukee, WI 53212 USA

Translation: Gini Holland
Gareth Stevens editor: Gini Holland
Gareth Stevens art direction and design: Tammy West

This edition copyright © 2007 by Gareth Stevens, Inc. Original edition copyright ©
2002 by Mango Jeunesse Press. First published as *Les animinis: Dans le jardin* by
Mango Jeunesse Press.

Printed in the United States of America

1 2 3 4 5 6 7 8 9 10 10 09 08 07 06